# THIS BOOK BELONGS TO...

| Name: | Age: |
|---|---|

| Favourite player: |
|---|

# 2022/2023

## My predictions...   Actual...

Town's final position:

|  |  |
|---|---|

Town's top scorer:

|  |  |
|---|---|

League One winners:

|  |  |
|---|---|

League One top scorer:

|  |  |
|---|---|

FA Cup winners:

|  |  |
|---|---|

EFL Cup winners:

|  |  |
|---|---|

## Contributors: Peter Rogers

# A TWOCAN PUBLICATION

©2022. Published by twocan under licence from Ipswich Town Football Club.

ISBN: 978-1-914588-66-2

**PICTURE CREDITS:** Match Day Images, Paul Macro, Action Images, Alamy and Press Association.

£10

# CONTENTS

# GOAL
## OF THE
# SEASON

**When it came to selecting Ipswich Town's Goal of the Season for 2021/22, there was only ever one serious contender - Bersant Celina's audacious chipped effort in the Blues' 2-1 home win over Crewe Alexandra in November 2021.**

The 2021/22 campaign was the Kosovan international midfielder's second loan spell at Portman Road having spent 2017/18 with Town on a season-long loan from Manchester City. Having been something of a star turn during his first spell at Town, his second coming - this time on loan from French side Dijon - sparked real enthusiasm among Town fans ahead of the 2021/22 season.

Celina's stunner was one of the best strikes seen at Portman Road for quite some time and came when Town were already a goal to the good against the Railwaymen.

**With the first-half in injury time, and the half-time whistle only seconds away, Celina brilliantly took down a George Edmundson long ball 25 yards out before spotting visiting goalkeeper Dave Richards off his line and then deftly chipping the Crewe custodian. To the delight and amazement of the Town fans in the Sir Alf Ramsey Stand, the ball irresistibly dropped just under the bar and into the top corner of the net to make it 2-0.**

It was a moment of sheer instinctive brilliance and a goal up there with any the talented Kosovan had scored in either of his spells with the Blues and was his fourth of a six-goal season.

Celina was presented with the award at the club's end-of-season awards event and, after playing in Town's final game of the season at home to Charlton Athletic he returned to his parent club. Having occurred in the first half of the season, his stunning goal could not really be classed as a parting gift but it will certainly live long in the memory of those who were inside Portman Road to have seen it so superbly executed.

# BERSANT CELINA

**NUMBER OF SEASONS WITH THE BLUES:**

**11**

**IPSWICH TOWN LEAGUE APPEARANCES:**

**340**

**IPSWICH TOWN LEAGUE GOALS:**

**53**

# LEGEND

## JASON DOZZELL

**IPSWICH TOWN ACHIEVEMENTS:**

Second Division title winners 1991/92

**MAJOR STRENGTH:**

A great ability to surge forward and score goals from midfield

**INTERNATIONAL ACTION:**

Jason was capped by England at U21 level as a Town player

**FINEST HOUR:**

Scoring both goals in a vital 2-1 home win over Derby County in March 1992 as Town closed in on promotion to the top flight

**Homegrown heroes Jason Dozzell and Kieron Dyer are two creative midfield players who both made a big impression at Portman Road before sealing big-money moves to the Premier League.**

Both players were clear match winners on their day and blessed with the skill and talent to turn games in Town's favour. With the ability to score goals and create chances for teammates, these two former Town stars were both real crowd favourites at Portman Road. Ironically, they both also returned to Town for a second spell with the club later in their careers. But who was the best? That's for you to decide and here are a few facts and figures from their time in blue and white to help you reach your conclusion...

**It's a tough call...!**

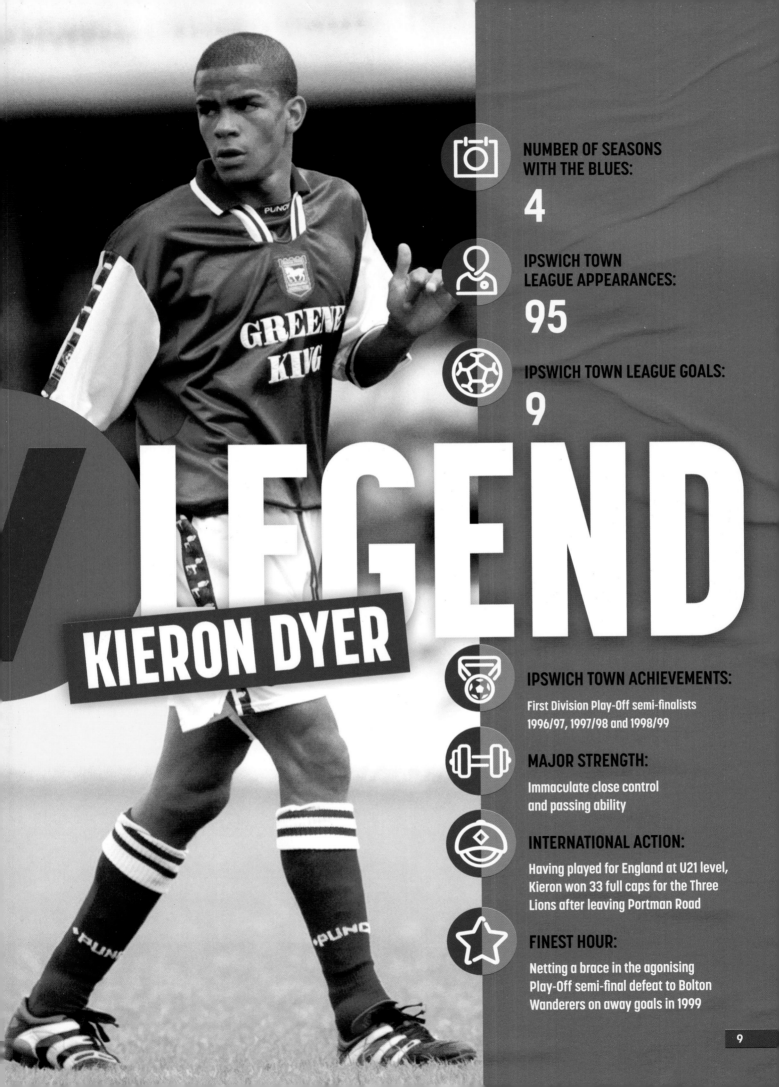

# LEGEND

## KIERON DYER

**NUMBER OF SEASONS WITH THE BLUES:**

**4**

**IPSWICH TOWN LEAGUE APPEARANCES:**

**95**

**IPSWICH TOWN LEAGUE GOALS:**

**9**

**IPSWICH TOWN ACHIEVEMENTS:**

First Division Play-Off semi-finalists 1996/97, 1997/98 and 1998/99

**MAJOR STRENGTH:**

Immaculate close control and passing ability

**INTERNATIONAL ACTION:**

Having played for England at U21 level, Kieron won 33 full caps for the Three Lions after leaving Portman Road

**FINEST HOUR:**

Netting a brace in the agonising Play-Off semi-final defeat to Bolton Wanderers on away goals in 1999

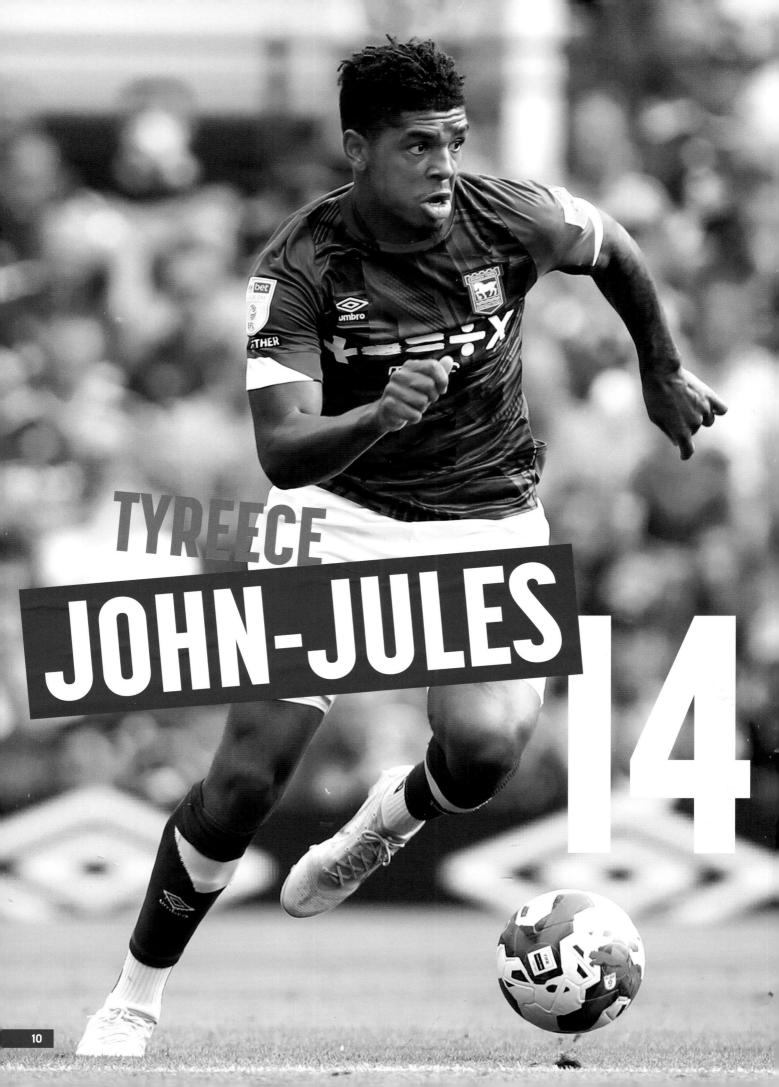

TYREECE
JOHN-JULES
14

10

Defending is not just about stopping the attackers and clearing your lines. Making the most of the possession you have just won is vital - although the danger has to be cleared, it is important for your team to keep hold of the ball.

# SOCCER
# SKILLS
## LONG PASSES

When passing your way out of defence, and short, side-foot passes are not possible, the longer pass driven over the heads of midfield players can be used.

## EXERCISE

In an area 40m x 10m, A1 and A2 try to pass accurately to each other with a defender B in the middle between them. Player B must attempt to stop the pass if possible, and A1 and A2 must keep the ball within the area of the grids.

After each successful long pass, the end player will exchange a shorter pass with B before passing long again, thus keeping the exercise realistic and also keeping the defender in the middle involved. The player in the middle should be changed every few minutes, and a 'count' of successful passes made for each player.

### KEY FACTORS

1   Approach at an angle.
2   Non-kicking foot placed next to the ball.
3   Eye on the ball.
4   Strike underneath the ball and follow through.

Practice is the key to striking a consistently accurate long pass and to developing the timing and power required.

The same end result could be achieved by bending the pass around the defender instead of over him, and this pass could be practised in the same exercise, by striking the football on its outer edge (instead of underneath) which will impart the spin required to make the ball 'bend' around the defender - not an easy skill!

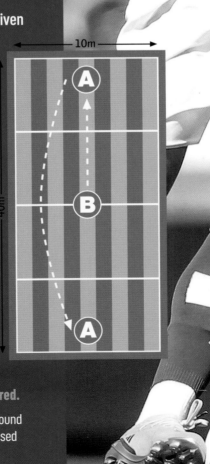

# LEAGUE ONE
## 2022/2023
# SQUAD

## 1 CHRISTIAN WALTON

GOALKEEPER DOB: 09/11/1995 BIRTHPLACE: ENGLAND

Town No.1 Christian Walton joined the Blues on loan from Premier League Brighton & Hove Albion in August 2021 and then made the move a permanent one in the 2022 January transfer window.

Already a firm favourite with the Town fans, Walton is a confident goalkeeper who commands his area and gives great confidence to those playing in front of him.

## 2 RICHARD KEOGH

**DEFENDER**  **DOB:** 11/08/1986  **BIRTHPLACE:** ROI

A vastly experienced central defender, Richard Keogh has seen his career go full circle as the one-time Ipswich Town trainee agreed a one-year deal at Portman Road in August 2022 - a day before his 36th birthday.

Keogh brings a great deal of knowledge and knowhow to the club's defensive ranks and is sure to offer both support and competition to his Town teammates.

## 3 LEIF DAVIS

**DEFENDER**  **DOB:** 31/12/1999  **BIRTHPLACE:** ENGLAND

Ipswich Town's ability to prise highly-rated left-back Leif Davis away from Premier League Leeds United in July 2022 was seen as a major coup for the Blues.

The 22-year-old featured in AFC Bournemouth's promotion-winning campaign for the Championship while on loan with the Cherries last season. He made his Town debut on the opening day of the current season in a draw with Bolton Wanderers.

## 4 GEORGE EDMUNDSON

**DEFENDER** **DOB:** 15/08/1997 **BIRTHPLACE:** ENGLAND

Central defender George Edmundson joined Town in July 2021 from Scottish Premier League side Glasgow Rangers when he put pen to paper on a four-year deal at Portman Road.

A powerful defender, who is comfortable in possession, Edmundson made 32 League One appearances for Town last season and scored his first goal for the club in the 6-0 victory over Doncaster Rovers at Portman Road.

## 5 SAM MORSY

**MIDFIELDER** **DOB:** 10/09/1991 **BIRTHPLACE:** EGYPT

Egyptian international midfielder Sam Morsy was the final Town signing of the busy 2021 summer transfer window and has since become captain.

A tough-tackling midfielder, who loves to make forward runs into attacking areas, Morsy is very much recognised as the heartbeat of the Town midfield. With two goals in the opening six games of Town's 2022/23 campaign, the skipper has begun the new season in outstanding form.

# LEAGUE ONE
## 2022/2023
# SQUAD

## 6 LUKE WOOLFENDEN

**DEFENDER** **DOB:** 21/10/1998 **BIRTHPLACE:** ENGLAND

**Ipswich-born central defender Luke Woolfenden has progressed through the Town Academy setup to establish himself as a first-team regular at Portman Road.**

A confident defender who is happy in possession and always looking to build play from the back, Woolfenden agreed a new four-year contract at Portman Road in the summer of 2020 and continues to excel with his hometown club.

## 7 WES BURNS

**MIDFIELDER** DOB: 23/11/1994 BIRTHPLACE: WALES

**Winger Wes Burns enjoyed an exceptional debut season with Ipswich Town in 2021/22 having joined the club from Fleetwood in the summer of 2021.**

He topped the club's scoring charts with 13 goals in all competitions and created countless chances for teammates with his pace down the right flank. Voted Town's Player of the Season, he capped off a memorable campaign at club level with a call-up to Wales' full international team.

## 8 LEE EVANS

MIDFIELDER  DOB: 24/07/1994  BIRTHPLACE: WALES

Forming an excellent partnership with skipper Sam Morsy in the Town engine room, Lee Evans was a big miss for the Blues in the final three months of last season when he was sidelined with injury.

A hat-trick hero in the 6-0 demolition of Doncaster Rovers last season, Evans returned to the team at the start of the current campaign and netted the club's first goal of the new season against Bolton Wanderers.

## 9 FREDDIE LADAPO

FORWARD  DOB: 01/02/1993  BIRTHPLACE: ENGLAND

A proven League One goalscorer following spells with Plymouth Argyle and Rotherham United, 29-year-old Freddie Ladapo joined Town as a free agent in the summer of 2022 following the expiry of his Rotherham contract.

Having helped the Millers to promotion from League One last season, Ladapo certainly knows what's needed to succeed at this level. He was another player to make his Town debut in the opening-day draw with Bolton Wanderers.

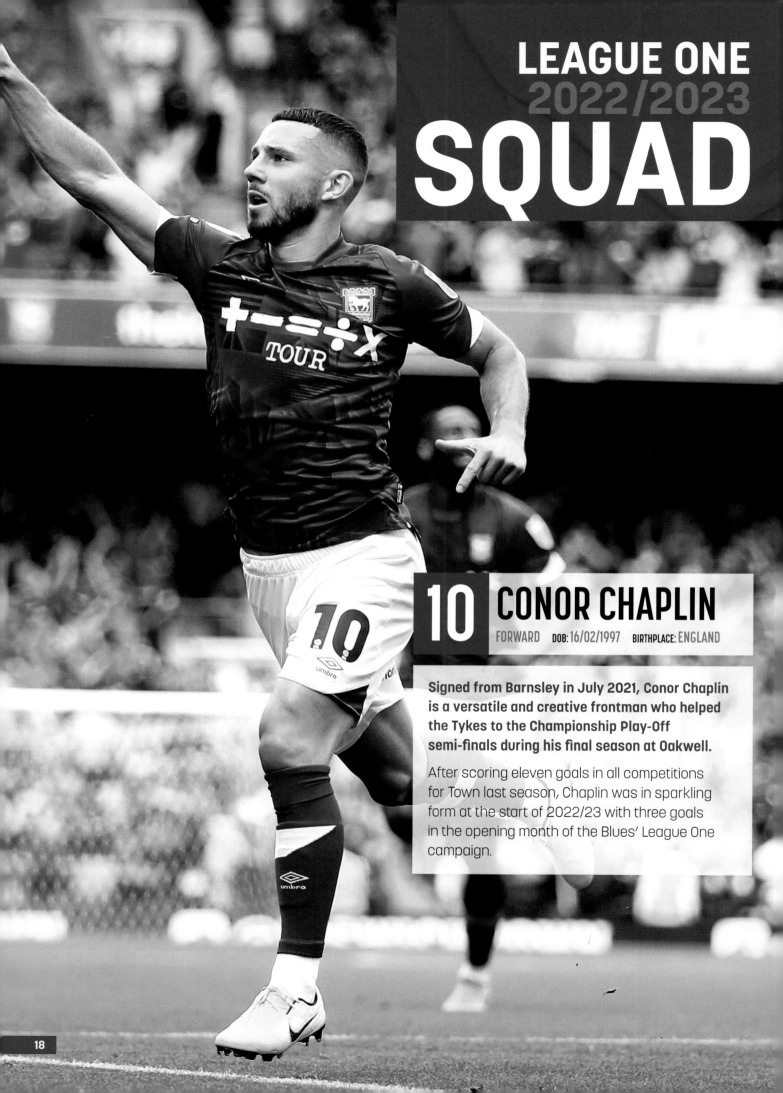

# LEAGUE ONE
## 2022/2023
# SQUAD

## 10 — CONOR CHAPLIN

**FORWARD**  **DOB:** 16/02/1997  **BIRTHPLACE:** ENGLAND

**Signed from Barnsley in July 2021, Conor Chaplin is a versatile and creative frontman who helped the Tykes to the Championship Play-Off semi-finals during his final season at Oakwell.**

After scoring eleven goals in all competitions for Town last season, Chaplin was in sparkling form at the start of 2022/23 with three goals in the opening month of the Blues' League One campaign.

## 11 MARCUS HARNESS

**MIDFIELDER** · DOB: 24/02/1996 · BIRTHPLACE: ENGLAND

**Attacking midfielder Marcus Harness signed a three-year deal with Town when he completed a transfer from League One rivals Portsmouth ahead of the current season.**

After scoring his first goal for the club in the 2-1 victory away to Forest Green in August, Harness then netted the only goal of the game to give Town all three points against his former club Burton Albion as Town made a flying start to the 2022/23 season.

## 12 DOMINIC BALL

**MIDFIELDER** · DOB: 02/08/1995 · BIRTHPLACE: ENGLAND

**A hard-working midfielder who is equally at home operating in a defensive role, Dominic Ball joined Town from Championship club Queens Park Rangers following the expiry of his contract at Loftus Road.**

A former Tottenham Hotspur academy player, his ball-winning ability and adaptability to play in a number of roles are sure to be a major asset for Town in our bid to win promotion from League One in 2022/23.

## 14 TYREECE JOHN-JULES

FORWARD  DOB: 14/02/2001  BIRTHPLACE: ENGLAND

An exciting forward player, Tyreece John-Jules joined Town in June 2022 on a season-long loan deal from Premier League giants Arsenal.

An England U21 international, John-Jules has previously gained valuable first-team experience with loan spells at Lincoln City, Doncaster Rovers, Blackpool and Sheffield Wednesday. The 21-year-old netted his first goal in Town colours in a 3-0 win away to Shrewsbury Town in August.

## 15 CAMERON BURGESS

DEFENDER  DOB: 21/10/1995  BIRTHPLACE: AUSTRALIA

A consistent performer in League One for Accrington Stanley, central defender Cameron Burgess moved to Portman Road in August 2021 when he agreed a three-year contract with the Blues.

Burgess made 27 appearances in all competitions last season and is happy to operate in a traditional back four or in a back three should the manager opt to change formation for certain fixtures.

## 19 KAYDEN JACKSON

**FORWARD** · **DOB:** 22/02/1994 · **BIRTHPLACE:** ENGLAND

A pacy forward who joined Ipswich in August 2018 from Accrington Stanley, Kayden Jackson looked all set to be ending his Portman Road career until he was handed a new lease of life by Kieran McKenna in the second half of last season.

Very much part of McKenna's plans for the team going forward, Jackson agreed a new deal with Town in the summer and will be keen to repay his manager's faith in him over the weeks and months ahead.

## 21 GREG LEIGH

**DEFENDER** DOB: 30/09/1994 BIRTHPLACE: JAMAICA

**Speedy left-back Greg Leigh was the third new face through the door at Portman Road ahead of the 2022/23 season.**

An attack-minded full-back, Leigh spent the 2021/22 season with League One rivals Morecambe and impressed the Portman Road faithful over the pre-season period and the early weeks of the new campaign with a number of polished performances.

## 23 SONE ALUKO

**FORWARD** DOB: 19/02/1989 BIRTHPLACE: NIGERIA

**Sone Aluko is now in his second season at Portman Road having joined Town on the eve of the 2020/21 campaign.**

Throughout an illustrious career Aluko has played in the Premier League, Championship and Scottish Premier League and brings a wealth of experience to the Town ranks. A valued member of the Town squad, 33-year-old Aluko featured in 30 League One fixtures for the Blues last season, scoring three goals.

# LEAGUE ONE
## 2022/2023
# SQUAD

## 24 KANE VINCENT-YOUNG

**DEFENDER** **DOB:** 15/03/1996 **BIRTHPLACE:** ENGLAND

Kane Vincent-Young joined the Blues in 2019 from neighbours Colchester United. The full-back made an instant impression at Portman Road, debuting in a 5-0 victory at Bolton Wanderers in August 2019 - he then netted his first Ipswich goal in a 1-0 victory over Gillingham a month later.

With the ability to power forward and support the attack, Vincent-Young has all the attributes of the modern-day defender. His time at Portman Road has been hampered by injuries and he will be keen to make up for lost time in 2022/23.

## 29 KYLE EDWARDS

**MIDFIELDER**   **DOB:** 17/02/1998   **BIRTHPLACE:** ENGLAND

**Tricky winger Kyle Edwards agreed a three-year deal with Ipswich Town in August 2021. The 24-year-old arrived at Portman Road following the expiry of his contract at West Bromwich Albion.**

Edwards had been with the Baggies since the age of six and progressed through the ranks to make 49 first-team appearances for Albion. He started 11 League One fixtures for Town last season and will be keen for more first-team opportunities in the current campaign.

## 30 CAMERON HUMPHREYS

**MIDFIELDER**   **DOB:** 30/10/2003   **BIRTHPLACE:** ENGLAND

**Teenage midfielder Cameron Humphreys is the latest star to emerge from the club's successful youth Academy.**

Handed a Town debut by former boss Paul Cook in last season's EFL Cup tie against Newport County, Humphreys made three other first-team appearances last season and was rewarded with a new three-year deal at Portman Road this summer. His first involvement in the current campaign came as Town faced local rivals Colchester United in the EFL Cup.

## 31 VACLAV HLADKY

GOALKEEPER  DOB: 14/11/1990  BIRTHPLACE: CZECH REPUBLIC

Ipswich signed Czech goalkeeper Vaclav Hladky from League Two Salford City in June 2021. The 31-year-old stopper agreed a three-year contract at Portman Road and has provided excellent cover and competition to Christian Walton.

Hladky initially arrived in the UK in 2019 when he played for Scottish side St Mirren but it was following an impressive spell at Salford that he landed on Town's radar.

## 44 JANOI DONACIEN

DEFENDER  DOB: 03/11/1993  BIRTHPLACE: ST LUCIA

Nobody made more League One appearances for Town last season than defender Janoi Donacien. The 28-year-old formed a great understanding down the right side with Wes Burns and his performances saw him push Burns all the way for the Player of the Season accolade.

Initially joining the Blues on loan from Accrington Stanley in the summer of 2018, before making the move a permanent arrangement in the 2019 January transfer window, he is now one of the club's longest serving players among the current squad.

**IPSWICH TOWN FOOTBALL CLUB**

# MULTIPLE CHOICE

Here are ten Multiple Choice questions to challenge your footy knowledge!

Good luck...

ANSWERS ON PAGE 62

**1.** What was the name of Tottenham Hotspur's former ground?

A) White Rose Park
B) White Foot Way
C) White Hart Lane

**2.** Which club did Steven Gerrard leave to become Aston Villa manager?

A) Liverpool,
B) Glasgow Rangers
C) LA Galaxy

**3.** Mohamed Salah and Son Heung-min were joint winners of the Premier League Golden Boot as the division's top scorers in 2021/22.

How many goals did they score?

A) 23   B) 24   C) 25

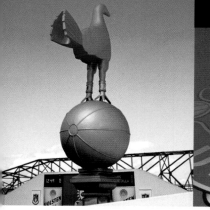

**4.** What is the nationality of Manchester United boss Erik ten Hag?

A) Swiss   B) Dutch
C) Swedish

**5.** Where do Everton play their home games?

A) Goodison Road
B) Goodison Way
C) Goodison Park

**6.** From which club did Arsenal sign goalkeeper Aaron Ramsdale?

A) Sheffield United
B) Stoke City
C) AFC Bournemouth

**7.** What is Raheem Sterling's middle name?

A) Shaun
B) Shaquille
C) Silver

**8.** Who won the 2021/22 League One Play-Off final?

A) Wigan Athletic
B) Sunderland
C) Rotherham United

**9.** How many times have Ipswich Town won the FA Cup?
A) Once
B) Twice
C) Three times

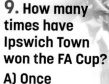

**10.** Which League Two club was Town defender Corrie Ndaba on loan at in 2021/22?

A) Newport County
B) Bradford City
C) Salford City

26

MARCUS

HARNESS

11

ANSWERS ON PAGE 62

# CLASSIC
# FAN'TASTIC

Bluey is hiding in the crowd in five different places as Ipswich Town fans celebrate winning the FA Cup at Wembley in 1978. Can you find all five?

WES
BURNS
7

Close control in tight situations creates havoc in opposition defences - particularly when receiving the ball in the air - and nine times out of ten, when a striker receives the ball, he has his back to goal.

# SOCCER SKILLS
## RECEIVING THE BALL

Quite often the ball will arrive in the air, and good strikers have to be able to cope with that - controlling and turning in one movement, ready for the instant shot.

## EXERCISE 1

In an area 20m x 10m, two players A and A2 test the man in the middle, B, by initially throwing the ball at him in the air, with the instruction to turn and play in to the end man - if possible using only two touches.

The middle player is changed regularly, and to make things more realistic, the end players progress to chipping the ball into the middle.

The middle player is asked to receive and turn using chest, thigh, or instep.

### KEY FACTORS

1  Assess flight early - get in position.
2  Cushion the ball.
3  Be half-turned as you receive.

## EXERCISE 2

A progression of this exercise is the following, where the ball is chipped or driven in to the striker from varying positions. He has to receive with his back to goal, and using just two touches in total if possible, shoot past the 'keeper into the goal!

To make this even more difficult, a defender can be brought in eventually. For younger children, the 'servers' should throw the ball to ensure consistent quality.

31

# TRAIN TO WIN

**Making sure that you are fit, healthy and fully prepared is key to success in whatever challenge you are taking on. Those three factors are certainly vital for professional footballers and also for any young aspiring player who plays for his or her school or local football team. The importance of fitness, health and preparation are key factors behind the work that goes into preparing the Ipswich Town players to perform at their maximum on matchday.**

Town players will need to demonstrate peak levels of fitness if they want to feature in Kieran McKenna's team. Before anyone can think of pulling on a blue shirt and stepping out at Portman Road, they will have to perform well at the training ground to have shown the manager, his coaches and fitness staff that they are fully fit and ready for the physical challenges that await them on a matchday.

**Regardless of whether training takes place at the training ground or at the stadium, the players' fitness remains an all-important factor. Of course time spent practicing training drills and playing small-sided games will help a player's fitness but there is lots of work undertaken just to ensure maximum levels of fitness are reached.**

Away from the training ground, the players will spend a great deal of time in the gymnasium partaking in their own personal workouts. Bikes, treadmills and weights will all form part of helping the players reach and maintain a top level of fitness.

Over the course of a week, the players will take part in many warm-up and aerobic sessions and even complete yoga and pilates classes to help with core strength and general fitness. The strength and conditioning coaches at the club work tirelessly to do all they can to make sure that the players you see in action are at their physical peak come kick-off.

While the manager and his staff will select the team and agree the tactics, analysts will provide the players and staff with details on the opposition's strengths, weaknesses and their likely approach to the match.

**Suffice to say the training ground is a busy place and no stone is left unturned in preparation for the big match!**

# PLAYER
## OF THE
# YEAR

## WES
## BURNS

**Flying wing-back Wes Burns enjoyed a highly impressive debut season at Portman Road which was capped off with a triple celebration at the end of the 2021/22 campaign.**

After joining from League One rivals Fleetwood Town in the summer of 2021, Burns wasted little time in making his mark for the Blues. Over the course of the season, the 27-year-old chipped in with 13 goals including braces in the 2-0 away win over AFC Wimbledon and the 4-0 rout of Charlton Athletic on the final day of the season.

Burns' double strike against the Addicks saw the Welshman end the season as Town's leading scorer but even before that he'd done enough to win the supporters' seal of approval when it came to voting for their 2021/22 Player of the Year. Burns topped the supporters voting with Janoi Donacien's consistent performances in the Blues' backline seeing him as runner-up.

**Picking up the prestigious Player of the Year award came just a few days after Burns' teammates had voted him the Players' Player of the Year at the club's end-of-season awards event. Unsurprisingly, the Town man's performances also landed him a place in the PFA League One Team of the Season.**

Once the dust had settled on the Blues' 2021/22 campaign, Burns' performances were rewarded with a call-up to the Wales national squad for the Red Dragons' three Nations League fixtures in June. Burns won his first international cap when he started Wales' Nations League match away to Poland on 1st June before tasting further international action against Belgium and the Netherlands. After Wales secured a place in the 2022 FIFA World Cup finals, which will take place this winter, Town's Welsh wizard now has his sights set on trying to win a place in Rob Page's squad for Qatar.

**Following a momentous season for club and country, Burns delighted Town fans without even having to kick a ball when he agreed a new long-term deal at Portman Road ahead of the 2022/23 campaign.**

# DREAM TEAM

Pick your ultimate Ipswich Town
dream team and design them a kit!

SAM
MORSY
5

## ACCRINGTON STANLEY
# SEAN McCONVILLE

Approaching 300 career appearances across two spells with the club, midfielder Sean McConville is a true Accrington Stanley legend.

A reliable performer and probably the first name on manager John Coleman's team-sheet, McConville has played a great part in helping Stanley secure a fourth consecutive season at League One level.

# DANGER MEN

THE OFFICIAL 2023 IPSWICH TOWN ANNUAL TAKES A LOOK AT 24 LEAGUE ONE STARS THAT COULD PERFORM VITAL ROLES FOR THEIR CLUBS DURING THE 2022/23 SEASON.

## BARNSLEY
# DEVANTE COLE

The son of former Newcastle United, Manchester United and England striker Andrew Cole, 27-year-old Devante Cole is now in his second spell with the Tykes having previously played on loan at Oakwell in 2014/15.

The striker netted five goals in 19 appearances when on loan from Manchester City and will be looking to establish a formidable partnership with new signing James Norwood at League One level in 2022/23.

## BRISTOL ROVERS
# JOHN MARQUIS

Following their dramatic final-day promotion to the third tier last season, Bristol Rovers completed the signing of expert League One marksman John Marquis.

A prolific goalscorer with Doncaster Rovers and Portsmouth, Marquis joined Rovers following a short-term deal with Lincoln City. With the ability to cause problems for defenders in the air or on the ground - his first Bristol Rovers goal secured a 1-0 victory over Oxford United earlier this season.

## BOLTON WANDERERS
# ELIAS KACHUNGA

A mobile and intelligent forward, Elias Kachunga made his mark in the UK with Huddersfield Town as the Terriers won promotion to the Premier League in 2016/17.

A full Congolese international, Kachunga joined Bolton from Sheffield Wednesday in 2021. Now in his second season at the club, the 30-year-old forward will have a key role to play over the coming months.

## BURTON ALBION
# DAVIS KEILLOR-DUNN

Burton Albion snapped up goalscoring midfielder Davis from Oldham Athletic in the summer of 2022 following the Boundary Park club's fall to the National League.

The 24-year-old midfielder scored 28 goals across two seasons with the Latics and opened his Albion account with a hat-trick in the opening month of the 2022/23 League One season as the Brewers drew 4-4 away to Accrington Stanley.

## CAMBRIDGE UNITED
# JOE IRONSIDE

Cambridge United striker Joe Ironside scored 15 goals last season, including an historic strike in Cambridge's shock 1-0 FA Cup victory over Premier League giants Newcastle United at St James' Park in January 2022.

The 29-year-old striker also bagged a hat-trick in the 5-0 League One win away to Cheltenham Town. Ironside is expected to be the team's main goal threat again in 2022/23.

## DERBY COUNTY
# DAVID McGOLDRICK

Derby County secured the signing of former Republic of Ireland international striker David McGoldrick in July 2022.

The arrival of such an experienced and proven goalscorer is sure to boost the Rams for their 2022/23 League One campaign. A skilful and intelligent forward, McGoldrick has great ability to link-up play in the final third and score goals too.

## CHARLTON ATHLETIC
# JAYDEN STOCKLEY

Former Preston North End striker Jayden Stockley moved to Charlton Athletic in the summer of 2021 having spent the previous six months on loan at The Valley.

He reached double figures in League One last season with 13 goals and netted his first of 2022/23 in the Addicks' 5-1 demolition of Plymouth Argyle in August 2022.

## EXETER CITY
# MATT JAY

Another young player to have emerged from the Exeter City academy, midfielder Matt Jay contributed a whopping 14 goals from midfield as the Grecians won promotion from League Two last season.

The most significant of his goals came in April 2022 as Barrow were defeated 2-1 with Jay netting the winning goal that secured promotion. A very highly rated performer, Jay will be keen to prove his worth at League One Level this season.

## CHELTENHAM TOWN
# ALFIE MAY

Striker Alfie May enjoyed a 26-goal season for Cheltenham Town in 2021/22 when his goals proved vital in the club maintaining League One status.

Of his 26 goals last season, 23 came in League One including a brace against former club Doncaster Rovers in a 4-0 victory - while in February 2022 he scored four goals in an amazing 5-5 draw with Wycombe Wanderers at Adams Park.

## FLEETWOOD TOWN
# HARVEY MACADAM

Plucked from National League North side Ashton United in the January 2022 transfer window, 21-year-old midfielder Harvey Macadam marked his full league debut with a goal in the Cod Army's 3-1 win at Crewe in April 2022.

Macadam will be out to impress new Fleetwood boss Scott Brown this season as he aims to make a first-team place his own in 2022/23.

## FOREST GREEN ROVERS
# JAMILLE MATT

Striker Jamille Matt netted 20 goals in all competitions last season as Forest Green Rovers won the League Two title and sealed a first promotion to the third tier.

The Jamaican front-man will form the focal point of the attack at the New Lawn in 2022/23 as Forest Green attempt to establish themselves at League One level.

## MK DONS
# BRADLEY JOHNSON

A vastly-experienced central midfielder, Bradley Johnson joined MK Dons in the summer of 2022.

His knowledge and knowhow are sure to be of great benefit to the younger players in the Dons' squad and the 35-year-old showed his new fans he still knows where the goal is as he scored twice to give Liam Manning's team their first win of the season when they defeated Port Vale in August.

## IPSWICH TOWN
# MARCUS HARNESS

Ipswich Town swooped on League One rivals Portsmouth for the services of goalscoring midfielder Marcus Harness in July 2022.

A very skilful and pacy winger, Harness can operate on either flank and his versatility is sure to be of great benefit to Kieran McKenna's side as they plan their 2022/23 League One campaign and push for automatic promotion to the Championship.

## MORECAMBE
# JONATHAN OBIKA

A product of the Tottenham Hotspur academy, striker Jonathan Obika was capped by England at both U19 and U20 level earlier in his career.

Obika joined Morecambe from St Mirren in June 2021 and his twelve appearances and two goals helped the Shrimpers maintain their third tier status last season. The 32-year-old will be keen for more games and goals in the current campaign.

## OXFORD UNITED
# JOSH MURPHY

A former FA Youth Cup winner and Premier League star with Norwich City and Cardiff City, winger Josh Murphy brings experience, pace and a real goal threat to the Oxford United League One promotion push.

A player capable of producing the spectacular, Murphy's arrival at the Kassam Stadium has been seen as a great coup for Oxford United.

## LINCOLN CITY
# TOM HOPPER

Forward Tom Hopper was handed the Lincoln City captaincy for the 2022/23 season by new boss Mark Kennedy.

A regular goalscorer at Sincil Bank since joining the Imps from Southend United in January 2020, Hopper started the current campaign in fine form with an opening-day goal against Exeter City and was then on target in Lincoln's 2-1 win at Oxford.

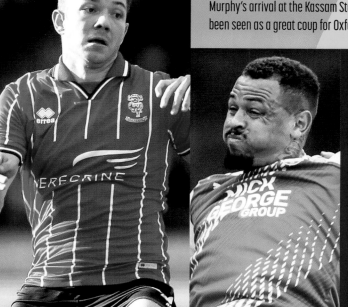

## PETERBOROUGH UNITED
# JONSON CLARKE-HARRIS

Proven League One marksman Jonson Clarke-Harris fired home 31 league goals in Posh's 2020/21 promotion-winning campaign.

His dozen Championship goals could not help United avoid the drop last season, but his form in front of goal will certainly prove vital to any success the London Road club enjoys.

## PLYMOUTH ARGYLE
# FINN AZAZ

Plymouth Argyle boosted their firepower for the 2022/23 League One campaign with the loan signing of highly-rated Aston Villa youngster Finn Azaz.

The 22-year-old attacking midfielder was on target three times in the opening month of the season for an Argyle side that harbour ambitions of at least a Play-Off place come the end of the campaign.

## SHEFFIELD WEDNESDAY
# MICHAEL SMITH

A summer signing from South Yorkshire rivals Rotherham United, striker Michael Smith is something of a League One promotion specialist having secured a hat-trick of promotions to the second tier while at the New York Stadium.

A prolific scorer at this level, Smith netted 25 goals in all competitions for the Millers last season and the Hillsborough faithful will be hopeful of a similar return in 2022/23.

## PORT VALE
# ELLIS HARRISON

Much-travelled centre-forward Ellis Harrison reunited with his former Bristol Rovers manager Darrell Clarke when he joined Port Vale at the start of the new 2022/23 season.

Harrison has great physical attributes and is an excellent League One target man - he netted his first Vale goals in back-to-back games against MK Dons and Burton Albion in August 2022.

## SHREWSBURY TOWN
# DANIEL UDOH

Forward Daniel Udoh hit the headlines in January 2022 when he scored to give Shrewsbury Town a shock lead in their FA Cup third round tie against Liverpool at Anfield.

The Nigerian forward scored 15 goals in all competitions for the Shrews last season and opened his account for current campaign in an EFL Cup tie against Carlisle United.

## PORTSMOUTH
# COLBY BISHOP

Recruited from League One rivals Accrington Stanley in July 2022, forward Colby Bishop has made a flying start to his Fratton Park career.

The 25-year-old netted a highly impressive five goals in his first five outings in a Portsmouth shirt including both goals in a 2-0 victory away to Cheltenham Town.

## WYCOMBE WANDERERS
# SAM VOKES

Former Wales international forward Sam Vokes brings power, strength and a wealth of experience to the Wycombe attack.

The 32-year-old scored 17 League One goals last season as the Chairboys' campaign to return to the Championship saw them reach the League One Play-Off final where they lost 2-0 to Sunderland at Wembley.

JANOI
DONACIEN
44

# TRUE OR FALSE?

Here are ten fun footy True or False teasers for you to tackle! Good luck...

ANSWERS ON PAGE 62

**2.** The FIFA World Cup in 2026 is due to be hosted in the USA, Mexico and Canada

**3.** Manchester City's former ground was called Maine Park

**1.** England star Harry Kane has only ever played club football for Spurs

**4.** Liverpool's Jurgen Klopp has never managed the German national team

**5.** Gareth Southgate succeeded Roy Hodgson as England manager

**6.** Manchester United's Old Trafford has the largest capacity in the Premier League

**7.** Jordan Pickford began his career at Everton

**8.** Huddersfield Town's nickname is the Terriers

**9.** Ipswich Town signed Marcus Harness from Plymouth Argyle

**10.** Wes Burns scored 12 League One goals for Town in 2021/22

43

**NUMBER OF SEASONS WITH THE BLUES:**

# 4

**IPSWICH TOWN LEAGUE APPEARANCES:**

# 75

**IPSWICH TOWN LEAGUE GOALS:**

# 27

**PLAYER OF THE SEASON WINNER:**

# 2000/01

# LEGEND
# MARCUS STEWART

**IPSWICH TOWN ACHIEVEMENTS:**

First Division Play-Off winners 1999/2000

**MAJOR STRENGTH:**

A lethal finisher in and around the penalty area and in one-on-one situations

**INTERNATIONAL ACTION:**

To the surprise of many Town fans, Stewart was never called up by England despite his impressive Premier League form in 2000/01

**FINEST HOUR:**

A Premier League hat-trick as Town defeated Southampton 3-0 at Portman Road in April 2001

**Strikers Marcus Stewart and Daryl Murphy both won the adulation of the Portman Road faithful as consistent goalscorers for Ipswich Town.**

Two impressive frontmen who led the Town attack and embraced the responsibility of being Ipswich's go-to men for goals throughout their Portman Road careers. While Stewart was feared for his excellent movement and clinical finishing, Murphy possessed a great physical presence and ensured that any central defender who was challenged with the task of marking him would certainly have known they'd been in a game.

Each player boasted an impressive goals-to-games ratio but who was the best? Well that's for you to decide and here are a selection of facts and figures from their time with Town to help you make your choice...

**Once again, it's a tough call...!**

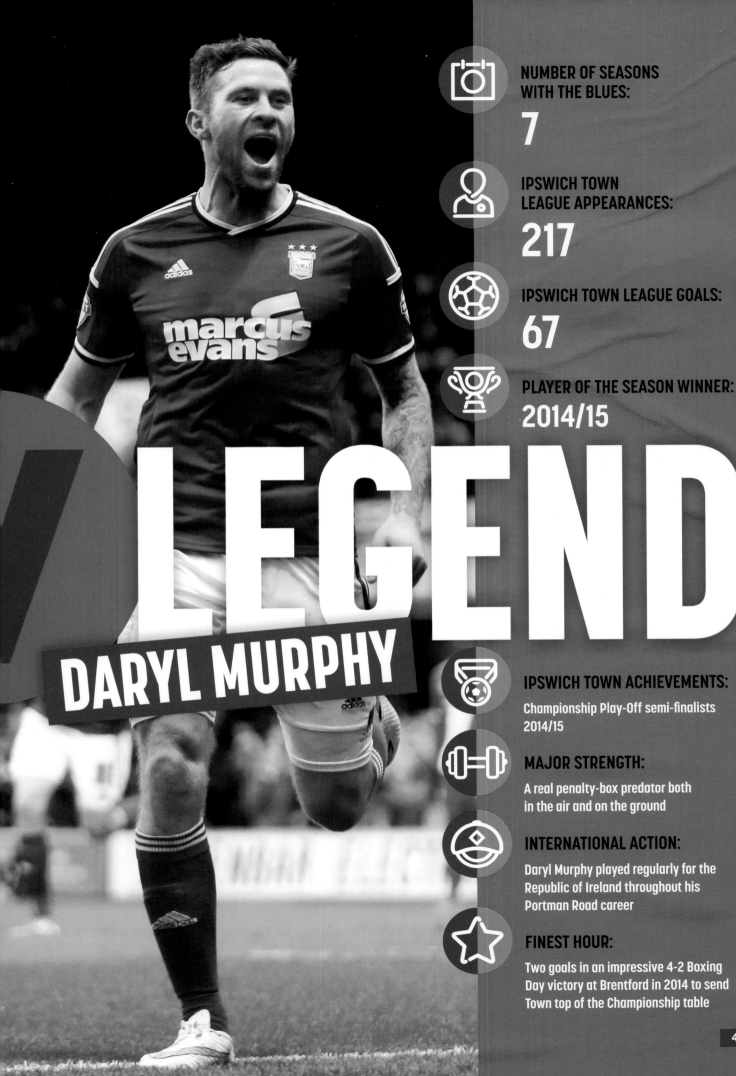

NUMBER OF SEASONS WITH THE BLUES:

7

IPSWICH TOWN LEAGUE APPEARANCES:

217

IPSWICH TOWN LEAGUE GOALS:

67

PLAYER OF THE SEASON WINNER:

2014/15

# LEGEND

## DARYL MURPHY

IPSWICH TOWN ACHIEVEMENTS:

Championship Play-Off semi-finalists 2014/15

MAJOR STRENGTH:

A real penalty-box predator both in the air and on the ground

INTERNATIONAL ACTION:

Daryl Murphy played regularly for the Republic of Ireland throughout his Portman Road career

FINEST HOUR:

Two goals in an impressive 4-2 Boxing Day victory at Brentford in 2014 to send Town top of the Championship table

# CLUB SEARCH

EVERY TEAM IN LEAGUE ONE IS HIDDEN IN THE GRID, EXCEPT FOR ONE... CAN YOU WORK OUT WHICH ONE?

```
M I L T O N K E Y N E S D O N S O B G S
Q J C S M Y E L S N R A B R L E X O W H
A F H H O N W O T H C I W S P I F L S E
G O A R H B F C U K T N I A C C O T R F
E R R E X E T E R C I T Y D H S R O E F
E E L W S N I V Y P H G Z Q E R D N R I
L S T S M O R E C A M B E V L E U W E E
Y T O B H I Y P D N M X A V T V N A D L
G G N U T B T S B M J L N I E O I N N D
R R A R U L N L K J E O N P N R T D A W
A E T Y O A U T I G N U O S H L E E W E
H E H T M N O L K M E R H U A O D R E D
T N L O S O C Z W G T P B Y M T S E B N
U R E W T T Y A D V R E P D T S B R M E
O O T N R R B I A Y A F G L O I F S O S
M V I B O U R L X V B A V M W R K D C D
Y E C F P B E N H Q L T C W N B J C Y A
L R P C M O D L I N C O L N C I T Y W Y
P S R A D N W O T D O O W T E E L F P W
A C C R I N G T O N S T A N L E Y S U I
```

Accrington Stanley

Barnsley

Bolton Wanderers

Bristol Rovers

Burton Albion

Cambridge United

Charlton Athletic

Cheltenham Town

Derby County

Exeter City

Fleetwood Town

Forest Green Rovers

Ipswich Town

Lincoln City

Milton Keynes Dons

Morecambe

Oxford United

Peterborough United

Plymouth Argyle

Port Vale

Portsmouth

Sheffield Wednesday

Shrewsbury Town

Wycombe Wanderers

ANSWERS ON PAGE 62

# CONOR CHAPLIN

10

# WHICH BALL?

Can you work out which is the actual match ball in these two action pics?

ANSWERS ON PAGE 62

# NAME THE SEASON

ANSWERS ON PAGE 62

Can you recall the campaign when these magic moments occurred?

Good luck...

IPSWICH TOWN
FOOTBALL CLUB

**1.** In which season did Chelsea last win the UEFA Champions League?

**2.** When were Manchester United last Premier League champions?

**3.** At the end of which season were England crowned World Cup winners?

**4.** In which season did Aleksandar Mitrovic net 43 Championship goals for Fulham?

**5.** In which season did Leicester City become Premier League champions?

**6.** When did Tottenham Hotspur last reach the League Cup final?

**7.** In which season were Sheffield United last promoted to the Premier League?

**10.** In which season did Ipswich Town last win at Wembley?

**8.** When did Manchester City win their first Premier League title?

**9.** During which season did Paul Lambert become Ipswich Town manager?

49

# IPSWICH TOWN FC
# WOMEN

After England's fantastic achievement in winning the woman's UEFA European Championships in the summer of 2022, the profile of girls and women's football continues to grow and grow.

It was not just the Lionesses who enjoyed an impressive 2021/22 campaign though, the Ipswich Town women's team also made great strides last season. Competing in the FA Women's National League, the Town women mounted a serious promotion push and were locked in a two-way battle for the title with Southampton women throughout the majority of 2021/22.

Under the management of Joe Sheehan, Town's women eventually ended their league campaign in third place behind champions Southampton women and runners-up Oxford United women. With only the division's winning team then going into a Play-Off match to win promotion to the FA Women's Championship, gaining promotion to the next level is a tough task. However, that certainly won't stop Sheehan's current squad looking to make it to the next level in 2022/23.

**Together with having a team competing at the right end of the league table, the Town women have also enjoyed impressive runs in the Women's FA Cup in recent seasons too. The team's success has seen crowds grow at the Goldstar Ground in Felixstowe where the women play their home fixtures.**
**More often than not the women's home games are played on Sundays with new fans always welcome along at the Goldstar.**

With the interest in the Ipswich women's first team on the up, the club continues to work in growing the women's game at all levels while providing a development pathway for young girls to benefit from.

**Full details of the Ipswich Town women's team and their 2022/23 fixtures can be found on the club's official website itfc.co.uk**

# IPSWICH TOWN WOMEN 2022/23

### GOALKEEPERS

**Leonie Jackson**
**Nina Meollo**
**Sarah Quantrill**

### DEFENDERS

**Maria Boswell**
**Lucy Egan**
**Summer Hughes**
**Abbie Jackson**
**Abbie Lafayette**
**Olivia Smith**
**Sarah Smith-Walter**

### MIDFIELDERS

**Sarah Brasero-Carreira**
**Anna Grey**
**Bonnie Horwood**
**Nia Evans**
**Eloise King**
**Lucy O'Brien**
**Sophie Peskett**
**Kyra Robertson**
**Blue Wilson**

### FORWARDS

**Zoe Barratt**
**Maddie Biggs**
**Natasha Thomas**

1. WHO AM I?

2. WHO AM I?

4. WHO AM I?

3. WHO AM I?

ANSWERS ON PAGE 62

# WHO ARE YER?

Can you figure out who each of these Blues stars is?

5. WHO AM I?

6. WHO AM I?

7. WHO AM I?

8. WHO AM I?

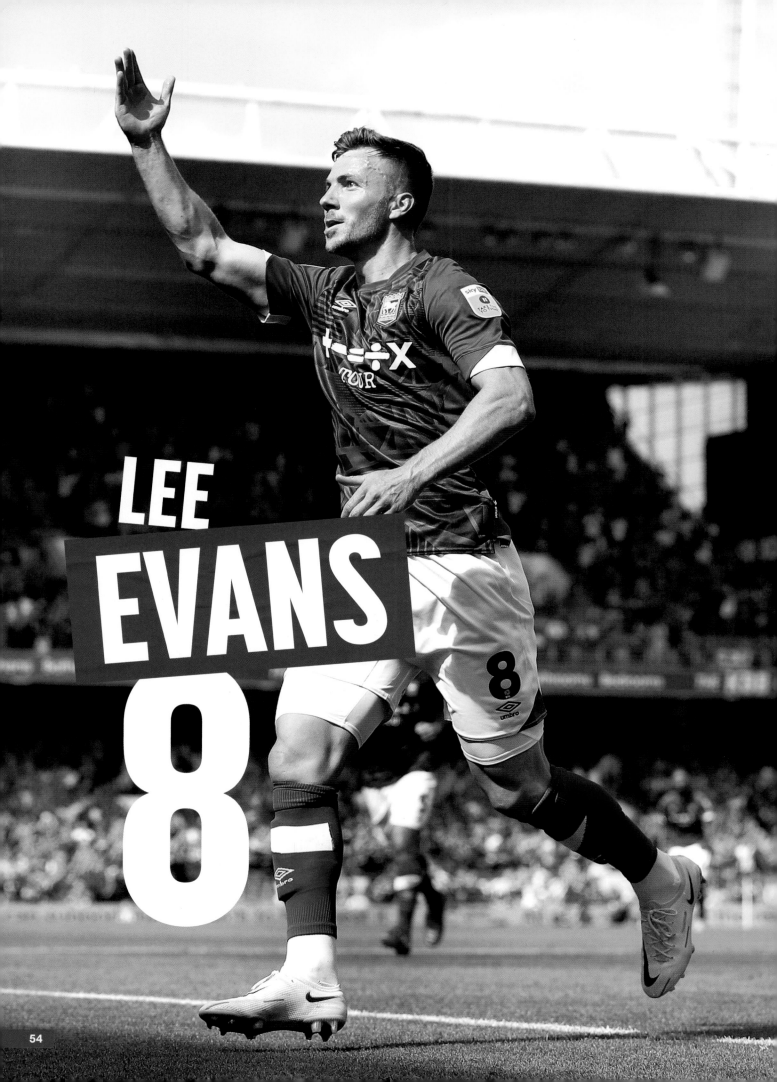

LEE
EVANS
8

# TRUE COLOURS

Can you colour in this picture of Lee Evans?

**PREMIER LEAGUE CHAMPIONS**
## Liverpool

# FAST FORWARD>>

Do your predictions for 2022/23 match our own?...

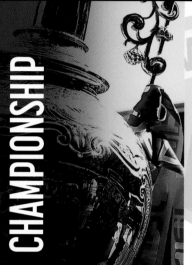

**CHAMPIONSHIP**

**CHAMPIONSHIP RUNNERS-UP**
## Watford

**PREMIER LEAGUE RUNNERS-UP**
## Chelsea

**PREMIER LEAGUE**

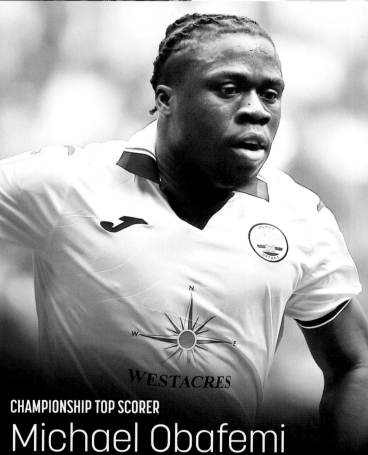

**PREMIER LEAGUE TOP SCORER**
## Erling Haaland

**CHAMPIONSHIP TOP SCORER**
## Michael Obafemi

**LEAGUE ONE TOP SCORER**
## Conor Chaplin

FA CUP

**FA CUP WINNERS**
## Spurs

**LEAGUE CUP WINNERS**
## Leicester City

LEAGUE CUP

**LEAGUE ONE CHAMPIONS**
## Ipswich Town

CHAMPIONS LEAGUE

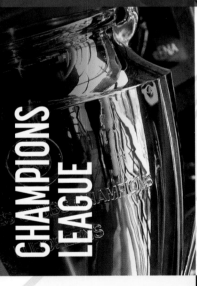

**CHAMPIONS LEAGUE WINNERS**
## Real Madrid

**LEAGUE ONE RUNNERS-UP**
## Oxford United

LEAGUE ONE

**EUROPA LEAGUE WINNERS**
## Roma

EUROPA LEAGUE

57

NUMBER OF SEASONS
WITH THE BLUES:

# 10

IPSWICH TOWN
LEAGUE APPEARANCES:

# 299

PLAYER OF THE SEASON WINNER:

# 2008/09

# LEGEND

## RICHARD WRIGHT

IPSWICH TOWN ACHIEVEMENTS:

First Division Play-Off semi-finalists
1996/97, 1997/98 and 1998/99

First Division Play-Off winners
1999/2000

MAJOR STRENGTH:

Superb reflexes to pull off smart
stops from point-blank range

INTERNATIONAL ACTION:

Richard won the first of his two full
England caps while a Town player

FINEST HOUR:

Saving a penalty in the 1999/2000
Play-Off final victory over
Barnsley at Wembley

**Two of Town's best 'keepers in the modern era, Richard Wright and Bartosz Bialkowski both starred in between the posts for the Blues.**

As the last line of defence, both Wright and Bialkowski produced a host of match-winning saves throughout their Portman Road careers while marshalling the defensive unit in front of them. While Bialkowski proved to be an inspired signing, Wright of course progressed though the club's youth ranks - but who was the best? It's a tricky one to decide and here are a number of facts and figures from their time at Portman Road to help you reach your decision...

**Yet again, it's certainly a tough call...!**

NUMBER OF SEASONS
WITH THE BLUES:

**5**

IPSWICH TOWN
LEAGUE APPEARANCES:

**168**

PLAYER OF THE SEASON WINNER:

**2015/16**
**2016/17**
**2017/18**

# LEGEND
## BARTOSZ BIALKOWSKI

IPSWICH TOWN ACHIEVEMENTS:

Championship Play-Off semi-finalists 2014/15

MAJOR STRENGTH:

Great command of the penalty area and confident collector of crosses

INTERNATIONAL ACTION:

Bartosz made his one and only international appearance for Poland during his Ipswich career

FINEST HOUR:

The 2016/17 season saw 'Bart' record a highly impressive eleven clean sheets

# IDENTIFY THE STAR

Can you put a name to the football stars in these ten teasers?

Good luck...

ANSWERS ON PAGE 62

**1.** Manchester City's title-winning 'keeper Ederson shared the 2021/22 Golden Glove award for the number of clean sheets with which Premier League rival?

**2.** Which Portuguese superstar re-joined Manchester United in the 2021/22 season?

**3.** Can you name the Brazilian forward who joined Aston Villa in May 2022 following a loan spell at Villa Park?

**4.** Who became Arsenal manager in 2019?

**5.** Who scored the winning goal in the 2021/22 UEFA Champions League final?

**6.** After 550 games for West Ham United, which long-serving midfielder announced his retirement in 2022?

**7.** Who took the mantle of scoring Brentford's first Premier League goal?

**8.** Who scored the final goal for Manchester City in their 2021/22 Premier League title-winning season?

**9.** Which player joined Ipswich from Brighton & Hove Albion in 2021/22?

**10.** Who joined Ipswich Town from Leeds United in July 2022?

# FREDDIE
## LADAPO
# 9

# ANSWERS

## PAGE 26 · MULTIPLE CHOICE

1. C. 2. B. 3. A. 4. B. 5. C. 6. A. 7. B. 8. B. 9. A. 10. C.

## PAGE 28 · FAN'TASTIC

## PAGE 43 · TRUE OR FALSE?

1. False, Harry played on loan for Leyton Orient, Millwall, Norwich City & Leicester City. 2. True. 3. False, it was called Maine Road. 4. True. 5. False, Gareth succeeded Sam Allardyce. 6. True. 7. False, Jordan began his career at Sunderland. 8. True. 9. False, he was signed from Portsmouth. 10. True.

## PAGE 46 · CLUB SEARCH

Peterborough United.

## PAGE 48 · WHICH BALL?

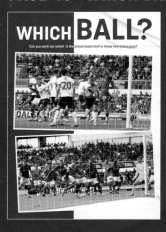

## PAGE 49 · NAME THE SEASON

1. 2020/21. 2. 2012/13. 3. 1965/66. 4. 2021/22. 5. 2015/16. 6. 2020/21. 7. 2018/19. 8. 2011/12. 9. 2018/19. 10. 1999/2000.

## PAGE 52 · WHO ARE YER?

1. Conor Chaplin. 2. Tyreece John-Jules. 3. Corrie Ndaba. 4. Dom Ball. 5. Lee Evans. 6. Luke Woolfenden. 7. George Edmundson. 8. Marcus Harness.

## PAGE 60 · IDENTIFY THE STAR

1. Allison Becker. 2. Cristiano Ronaldo. 3. Philippe Coutinho. 4. Mikel Arteta. 5. Vinicius Junior. 6. Mark Noble. 7. Sergi Canos. 8. Ilkay Gundogan. 9. Christian Walton. 10. Leif Davis.